Marjory Stoneman Douglas

and the

Florida Everglades

by

Sandra Wallus Sammons

Tailored Tours Publications
Box 22861
Lake Buena Vista, Florida 32830

Dedication

To Jeanne S. Bachman
An inspiration to the children
she teaches and a
joyful lover of nature.

Author's Acknowledgments

With deep appreciation to Marjory Stoneman Douglas for meeting with the author during her research. Thanks also to my mother, Elsie Wallus, for her careful reading of the manuscript and to the teachers and students who have consistently been involved in the development of my books.

Special thanks are also offered to the following: David Carr for his remembrances of the friendship between Marjorie Harris Carr and Mrs. Douglas; Sandy Dayhoff, Everglades National Park; Claudine Laabs for her exceptional cover photography; Sara Lee, educator and editor for her comments; Joette Lorion and Jim McMasters of the Friends of the Everglades; Robin Mitchell, Executive Director of the Florida Defenders of the Environment; Joe Podgor, a longtime friend of Mrs. Douglas; and Joan Morris and Joanna Norman of the Florida Photographic Archives.

First Edition

ISBN 1-892629–00-3

Foreword

She was a small woman, about five feet tall, living in a cottage she designed. Her home was almost hidden behind tropical plants on a quiet street in Coconut Grove, Florida. In her older years, she was almost blind.

This woman made a giant difference in helping people understand more about the environment. She had strong beliefs and a strong voice. Her words would be read and heard throughout Florida and around the world.

Marjory Stoneman Douglas has been called the "Grandmother of the Everglades," a "Champion," and a "Legend." Why? Her intelligent voice, leading many others, helped protect a mysterious land that was being destroyed. Her efforts helped save birds, wildlife, plants, and people that lived and thrived upon a wet, grassy, and beautiful land.

"There are no other Everglades in the world." That was the first sentence of Marjory's book entitled *The Everglades: River of Grass*. Her book taught people about the area west of Miami, Florida. She emphasized that the Everglades were not a swamp to be drained or paved. Instead, they were a "river of grass," part of a natural ecosystem that supplied fresh, clean water to south Florida.

Forceful when necessary, and always fearless when she knew she was right, Marjory talked about the importance of the Everglades to everyone who would listen. *The Everglades: River of Grass* was published when she was 57 years old. However, the period from when she was about 80 until well beyond her 105th birthday were her prime years of speaking for the Everglades.

Marjory Stoneman Douglas, 1958

Wearing her favorite red, floppy, wide-brimmed, "fighting" hat, Marjory made speech after speech. She was, to the last, an environmental pioneer working for the Everglades. As she put it:

We can still bring back much beauty to a changed and recreated earth.

Marjory Stoneman Douglas died a month after her 108th birthday. Were she still here, her comment to all of us would probably be to work even harder for the Everglades. She would say *"Let's get on with it!"*

Table of Contents

A Moment of Silence in the Florida Everglades

Chapter 1.

Discovering Her World

A young woman and her friend walked to the end of the road. Around them, they knew, were alligators, snakes, and perhaps even panthers. They were in the hot, wet, Florida Everglades. Everything was so quiet. Then, all of a sudden, there was a roaring sound.

What could be happening? They looked up and saw hundreds of birds take off in flight. The beautiful white creatures flew around and around in a large circle in the sky. All this was happening right in front of them and they stayed very still. When the first group of birds landed, another large group flew into the air—almost as if there had been a signal. The fascinating dance in the sky happened again and again. At last, the movement of the birds stopped.

The two people looked at each other in awe. They could hardly believe what they had seen.

During earlier walks in the mysterious Everglades, they had seen many birds, but they had *never* seen anything like this. After some time, the friends walked back along the roadway. The Everglades were still, as though nothing had happened.

Marjory Stoneman Douglas and her friend returned to Miami, where they learned they had witnessed what very few people would ever see. They had watched the mating flight of the white ibis. It happened to be the time of year when this beautiful white bird began its courtship ceremony. The birds leap up into the air in a thrilling dance before building their nests and hatching their young.

Marjory could hardly wait to go into the Everglades again. Exploring there was ever so much different from walks she had taken with her mother when she was a child. Marjory had lived where winters were cold and had not known about the variety of wildlife and plants that existed in the sunny, hot Everglades.

*****

The Minneapolis, Minnesota winter of 1889–1890 was cold and snowy. When April finally arrived, young Frank and Lillian Stoneman were happy for several reasons: they knew that they would soon have a new baby and they looked forward to milder weather so they could take their child for walks near the beautiful lakes.

Marjory Stoneman was born in Minneapolis on April 7,1890, over 1,000 miles north of the Everglades. She had no brothers or sisters. As a youngster, she spent a lot of time with her parents and other Minnesota relatives.

Her mother, Lillian, loved playing many musical instruments. She could play the guitar, the banjo, and the violin. She could even place glasses in a row and use different sized small sticks to play a tune. Perhaps because of her mother's interest, Marjory also enjoyed music.

Lillian Stoneman, 1880s

Frank Bryant Stoneman read to his young daughter. She loved his stories and books. As she grew, he taught Marjory to always think clearly and creatively. He wanted her to question whatever she saw or heard, as he had been trained to do by his own parents. Perhaps because of her father's love of books and language and reasoning, Marjory also enjoyed reading, writing, and clear, creative thinking.

Her father's relatives also lived in Minneapolis. They, too, enjoyed being with young Marjory and told her many family stories.

Marjory with her parents, 1893

Marjory learned that her grandfather, Mark Davis Stoneman, had been a doctor in the mid–1800s. He had strong beliefs and was always willing to work toward what he felt was right. Dr. Stoneman believed men should not go to war. However, he felt even more strongly that slavery was not right. For this reason, he became a surgeon for the Northern forces during the Civil War.

Marjory also was told about her great–great–uncle and aunt, Levi and Kate Coffin. They, too, had strong feelings that slavery was wrong. During the Civil War, the Coffins were part of a network of people who helped slaves escape to the North using what was called the "Underground Railroad." Although it was not really a railroad and it was not underground, it seemed like one because slaves who were running away would go from place to place, almost like going to and from stations along an invisible train track. People at each "station" would hide the slaves in their homes or barns, until they finally reached freedom. The Coffins, and many others, risked their lives to do what they believed to be right and to help others.

Marjory listened to the many stories about her family with a sense of pride. She learned that if people have strong beliefs and are willing to work hard, their lives can make a difference. Each person can help to make the world a better place.

Chapter 2.

A Caring Family

Although Florida would become Marjory's home when she was an adult, her first look at the state came when she was about four years old. Her parents planned a steamer trip to Havana and took Marjory with them. They stopped in Tampa, Florida. Many years later, Marjory remembered the "wonderful white tropic light." She also clearly recalled being lifted into the air so she could pick a fresh orange from a tree on the grounds of the Tampa Bay Hotel.

The Stoneman family moved to Rhode Island where her father started a business. When the business failed, however, it became too much for Marjory's mother. She became sick and decided she could not stay in Rhode Island with her husband any longer. Because of her illness, she needed to be close to people who could care for her and her daughter.

One day, when Marjory was only five, Lillian stuffed their clothes, books, and Marjory's toys into a suitcase. She helped Marjory into her hat and jacket. Holding the little girl's hand, Lillian walked out of the house and went to the train station. They boarded a train to Taunton, Massachusetts, the town where Lillian had grown up and where her parents still lived. By the time they arrived, the two travelers were hungry and tired. Lillian rang the doorbell and they were taken inside. Taking one look at her, Daniel and Florence Trefethen realized that their daughter was seriously ill. From that day on, they took loving care of their daughter and granddaughter.

Frank understood that Lillian's parents were helping, yet for a long time he kept hoping she would get better and come back. He missed his wife and their bright, funny little girl. However, as time passed, he realized Lillian and their child needed to stay with her parents. Marjory missed her father, but became increasingly close to her mother. Together they would often go for quiet walks around the neighborhood.

Marjory found that her mother's family was interesting, too. Her great–great–grandfather sailed the oceans. He once went from Maine, around the tip of South America, and then on to China. Marjory's great–grandfather, also a sailor, visited several cities in Europe before he was lost in a typhoon. Her grandfather was not a sailor. He went into business in Taunton and it was there that Marjory's mother was born. These relatives spoke French and told Marjory stories about France and taught her some French words.

Marjory learned to read when she was in first grade. She soon decided that reading was much more fun than playing with her dolls. In their home and at the nearby public library, she was surrounded by books. Marjory's imagination and curiosity about her world grew and grew. She later said:

You couldn't drag me away from books
or books away from me.

Marjory read anything she could find. She remembered most of what she read.

A magazine for children named *St. Nicholas* was particularly fun for Marjory. Filled with easy–to–read stories and articles, the magazine encouraged its readers to send in their own writing. One day Marjory invented a puzzle. She sent it to the magazine. Imagine her surprise when she learned that she had won the *St. Nicholas* Gold Medal. Marjory liked knowing that something she had created was in print for other children to enjoy.

Winning the contest was exciting for Marjory, but there were times when her childhood was sad. Her mother continued to be ill, and Marjory spent a lot of time trying to make Lillian's life happier. When she got home from school, they would play cards or little games, or perhaps just sit and talk. They did everything they possibly could together.

Marjory did well in school, and her sixth grade teacher, Miss Dartt, talked with her family about college. Miss Dartt hoped that they would send Marjory to the school that she had attended, Wellesley College. Marjory's mother and the rest of her family wanted her to continue her education. When the time came, they encouraged Marjory to send in her application. Marjory was concerned about leaving her mother, but she, too, wanted to go to college. She applied to Wellesley College and was accepted. The school, then only for women, was located in Wellesley, Massachusetts, near Boston. It was not very far from her home in Taunton.

Then, as now, a college education was expensive. Marjory's Aunt Fanny and her grandmother were determined to help, even though they did not have much money. Her aunt took on extra jobs and her grandmother probably used some of the housekeeping money to pay Marjory's bills. The family even rented out a room in their house for a time so that there would be enough money to keep Marjory in school.

Marjory later spoke about her aunt's and her grandmother's efforts to make sure she could complete her education. She said:

This was a sacrifice for which I could never thank them enough.

Chapter 3.

Out on Her Own

$\mathcal{M}$arjory liked many of her college courses, but she especially enjoyed English composition. She was quite sure she wanted to become a writer. Marjory also liked the public speaking courses. When the students practiced their speeches, she remembered that they had to project their voices. They had to:

> *. . . holler so loud we could hit the back of the auditorium.*

One of the courses that would make a difference to the rest of her life, however, was not in the English Department. It was a fascinating course in geography where she learned about rivers, mountain ranges, and oceans and how they were formed. Most important, however, Marjory learned that if one part of nature was changed, it could affect the balance and harmony of the rest of the earth. In later years, she remembered the lessons of that class well and said:

> *People need to take care of the earth and live in harmony with nature.*

She thought of her mother every day, and her grandmother's going–away present of a stack of

postcards came in handy. From when she arrived at Wellesley until her graduation four years later, Marjory wrote a note to her mother every single day.

Marjory Graduates from Wellesley College, 1912

Soon after graduation, Marjory's mother died. Marjory missed her mother very much, but she knew she had done her best to make Lillian's last years happy. After spending some time in Taunton with her family, Marjory was ready to begin her own career.

Although she really wanted to be a writer, Marjory knew how difficult it was for a young author to make a living. After all her family had done to help her through college, Marjory decided it was important to earn enough to support herself. She was accepted into a training program in a department store in Boston, Massachusetts. Soon after completing the classes, she moved to St. Louis, Missouri where one of her college friends lived and Marjory soon found work there. After a while, Marjory moved again. This time she went to Newark, New Jersey and worked at another department store. Although she was earning a living, Marjory did not enjoy her work. A library across the street helped, but she was not happy.

One day, a friend introduced Marjory to an interesting man. His name was Kenneth Douglas. He was at least 30 years older than Marjory, but she was attracted by his good looks and manner. As an editor of the Newark *Evening News*, Kenneth knew many people. Suddenly Marjory wasn't lonely any more. She and Kenneth went many places together and, about three months later, they were married.

The new marriage was happy for only a short time. One day Kenneth was arrested. The police said he had passed a bad check and sent him to jail for six months. Marjory waited for him, but she knew their marriage would never be the same.

Frank hadn't seen his daughter in many years. He heard the news about Kenneth and was worried about Marjory. Frank invited her to come to Miami, Florida to live with him and his second wife, Lillius, whom everyone called Lilla. They decided to send Marjory some money for a ticket for the long train trip south. Marjory also knew that she needed to

The Miami Train Station, ca. 1920s

Miami Street Scene
East on Flagler Street from Miami Avenue, September, 1915

divorce Kenneth and start a new life. In 1915, at the age of 25, she bought a blue dress, packed her bags, and took the train to Miami.

Chapter 4.

A New Life in Florida

It was a bright, sunny morning when Marjory stepped off the train. Her father met her at the station. When they arrived at Frank's house, Lilla, her new stepmother, gave Marjory a warm welcome. Marjory greatly enjoyed her new–found friendship with her father. Lilla soon became Marjory's best friend in Florida. How wonderful it was to be with family again.

The city of Miami did not impress Marjory right away. In 1915, it was a small city, but it was growing quickly. Marjory was surprised when she realized that there was not even a public library. The only library was at the Miami Woman's Club.

What she did love was the countryside. It caught her attention because it was so different from what she knew. She immediately liked the flat land; the great, bright sky; and the excitement of being in what was for her a whole new world.

Frank and Lilla's house was not fancy on the outside, but there were many treasures inside. Her father's collection of books lined the walls and helped make Marjory feel right at home. Lilla's interesting family history surrounded her. A beautiful dining table in the middle of one room was once owned by Thomas Jefferson, the third President of the United States. An attractive silver pitcher had belonged to Francis Eppes, one of the earliest mayors of Tallahassee, Florida's capital city. Mayor Eppes was given the pitcher because he created the first police force in Tallahassee. The police force helped make the rough frontier town of Tallahassee safer for its pioneer settlers and citizens.

These treasured pieces were important to Frank and Lilla not just because they were old, but because Lilla Stoneman was a relative of these famous men. She was a granddaughter of Francis Eppes and Francis Eppes was Thomas Jefferson's grandson. Marjory had again moved into a home where people were proud of their ancestors, where history and learning were important.

Frank Stoneman told his daughter all about his life since they had been together. After trying several businesses, he decided to study law. He moved from Rhode Island to Orlando, in central Florida, where he met Lilla. He then moved farther south to Miami and Lilla joined him.

When Frank moved to Miami it was still a small town, but changes had already started. Beginning in the late 1800s, shortly before Marjory's birth, a businessman named Henry Flagler visited

Florida. Henry began building a railroad and luxury hotels down the east coast of Florida, but had not decided to continue the railroad past Palm Beach. A woman named Julia Tuttle heard of his plans. She worked to convince him that Miami would be a perfect place for a railroad station and one of his luxury hotels. The Florida East Coast Railway soon stretched from Jacksonville to Miami—and then, some time later, would continue on to Key West.

Miami soon became one of the most important cities where Henry's trains stopped. When he decided to put the railroad station in Miami, Julia gave him some land and he bought even more. The land was used to build the railroad, the magnificent Hotel Royal Palm, houses, churches, a school, and more. In many ways, Julia Tuttle and Henry Flagler changed the city's future. When people realized Henry was interested in Miami, they also began to buy land. Suddenly, many people moved to the little city and it began to grow, perhaps too quickly.

As Frank Stoneman saw changes taking place, he realized some of the growth was good. However, in his opinion, some changes were not well planned and were happening too quickly. Homes and businesses were built everywhere. Perhaps, Frank thought, he could make a difference.

With an old flatbed printing press, Frank started a newspaper. As the first morning newspaper in the city, the Miami *News Record* attracted many readers. His strong beliefs about booming, out of control growth were the theme of many of the articles he wrote. Frank was particularly concerned about what was happening to the Everglades, a large, grassy, wetland to the west of Miami. People had started draining water from the Everglades. Frank thought that should not happen until the Everglades were better understood. Although many of Frank's ideas were sound, people became tired of the way his opinions were expressed. Enough people stopped buying the *News Record* that it had to close.

But Frank would not be silenced. In 1910, five years before Marjory arrived in Miami, he and a friend, Frank Shutts, created another newspaper. They named it the Miami *Herald* and Frank became its senior editor. From that day in 1910 when the first issue was printed, the *Herald* became an important voice of the "right thing to do." It became the public conscience of the city.

As Miami grew, the paper grew larger and larger. It reached more readers. Frank definitely was making a difference. His ideas helped people think about their city, its environment, and the way they, *the Miami residents,* wanted growth to happen.

Chapter 5.

Marjory Becomes a Writer

*W*hen Marjory arrived in Florida, her father needed good writers for the rapidly growing Miami *Herald*. At 25 years of age, Marjory was ready to begin the career she had wanted since her college days. She became a writer for the newspaper.

Her first assignment was as a part-time writer for the society column. Since it was a temporary position, Marjory did not have a desk at the paper. Instead, she worked from the house and a boy on a motorcycle came by to pick up her articles. In the society column, Marjory wrote about what Miami's wealthy residents and visitors were doing and thinking. She said:

> *I was delighted to be working on the Herald. It was as if everything else that I had been doing since college had been all wrong and suddenly I found what I was meant to do ... I didn't care what I was writing about as long as it was writing.*

The society editor job soon became full–time for Marjory. When that happened, she began to work in an office at the *Herald*. Frank taught his daughter the art of writing for a newspaper. He emphasized how important it was to get *all* the facts exactly correct.

The society column was full of news when Henry Flagler's Hotel Royal Palm opened each season on New Year's Day. However, all through the year there was something interesting and exciting going on in growing Miami. Marjory quickly learned a lot about writing, the newspaper business, and her adopted city.

Because Marjory was getting to know many people in Florida, she was asked to travel to Tallahassee with several other Florida women to speak out for women's suffrage. In 1916, when Marjory was 26, women in Florida were not allowed to vote in public elections. That spring, the five women spoke to legislators. Marjory recalled that those Florida law makers:

> *. . . never paid attention to us at all. They weren't even listening.*

Marjory would soon learn how to help people listen. She later said that Florida was the last state in the union to pass the amendment to the Constitution giving women the right to vote.

At that time, the front pages of newspapers all across America were filled with stories about

World War I which was then being fought in Europe. In Miami and elsewhere men volunteered to serve in the Army or the Navy. Women also wanted to help in the war effort, but they could not become soldiers or sailors. Instead, many joined the Army Reserve or the Naval Reserve or the American Red Cross.

One of Marjory's writing assignments was to interview the first woman from Miami to sign up to become a member of the Naval Reserve. She arrived early to talk with the Naval officers in order to get background information for the story. Marjory listened carefully to what they said. She heard about the need for workers for the war effort. Imagine everyone's surprise, perhaps including her own, when, on the spot, she signed up as the first woman recruit from Miami. At the time, she thought:

> *You have to stand up for some things in this world.*

Although her year with the Naval Reserve was over in 1918, when she was 28, the war was still going on. Once again, Marjory volunteered to help. This time she joined the American Red Cross. Her assignment was to write articles and she was soon sent to Paris, France. When she knew where she would be going, memories of her Grandmother

Trefethen's stories came back to her. She recalled the French words she had learned as a child. Marjory taught herself the French language so she would be able to talk with the French people she would meet. Even during the difficult and sometimes frightening war years, she loved France and, especially, Paris.

There was a balcony outside Marjory's Red Cross office in Paris. One day she was looking down at the quiet street below. Suddenly, there was the loud, banging sound of guns being fired. And then, almost immediately, came the clang of bells ringing from church towers across Paris. People ran into the streets shouting, "The War is over! The War is over!" Everyone in the Red Cross office joined the loud and happy celebration.

Even after the war, Marjory stayed with the Red Cross and continued writing. Her assignments took her all over France and to several other countries, including Greece and Italy. She was seeing more of the world and becoming a skilled writer.

In January, 1920, Marjory returned to Miami. Frank had written to her asking her to become assistant editor of the *Herald* at a salary of $30 a week. In only 36 months, little Miami had doubled in size. Marjory could hardly believe the changes. Everywhere she looked there was something new.

Chapter 6.

Speaking Out

There were also many changes at the Miami *Herald*. The newspaper, like the city, had grown. As assistant editor, Marjory wrote a column where she expressed her own ideas. It was called the *Galley*. In that section of the paper she wrote articles, stories, and poems. Marjory also worked on the editorial page. There were many days when she did three or four different jobs, all of which had to be finished accurately and quickly so the paper could go to press on time.

Since she sometimes wrote about the Everglades in her column, Marjory learned more about the area, its plants, and its geography. The more she wrote about the Everglades, the more convinced she became of their importance. Like her father, she was concerned about how south Florida's and Miami's growth would affect the Everglades and its water, wildlife, and plants.

Because of her growing interest in the Everglades, Marjory was introduced to David and Marian Fairchild. They knew a great deal about plants that grow in the south. David Fairchild became the head of a committee that wanted to protect the Everglades and make them a national park. Marjory was asked to be part of the committee.

Her future was beginning to unfold. Marjory was taking the opportunity to write and speak out for things she believed were right.

One day, she heard about a man named Martin Tabert, a poor vagrant, or wanderer. He had come to Florida from North Dakota, looking for a job. Before he could find work, he was arrested and sentenced to serve time in a labor camp. In those days, if a foreman didn't think a prisoner was working hard enough, the foreman could beat the prisoner with a whip. Martin Tabert was severely whipped and died from the terrible beating.

Marjory was shocked. The fact that it was legal to whip a person was just not right. She wrote a poem about Martin and his death. It was published in her column, the *Galley*. People in Miami read the poem. They talked about what had happened with their friends and neighbors. Soon, legislators in Tallahassee read her words. Not long after, they passed a law forbidding labor camp beatings. Marjory's words had made a difference.

Marjory later said she felt writing about Martin Tabert was the most important thing she had ever done.

Chapter 7.

Two Changes

Although Marjory's days at the Miami *Herald* kept her busy, she still made time to enjoy south Florida. She and her friends sometimes explored the fantastic beauty of the Everglades. It was early one morning that they saw the white ibis flying and doing their beautiful mating ceremony.

Each time Marjory went into the Everglades, she saw and learned new things. She saw alligators sunning themselves on dry spots of land. In the Ten Thousand Islands, at the southern edge of the Everglades, she sometimes saw 30,000 to 40,000 birds at one time. To Marjory, the Everglades were exciting and mysterious. They were a place where nature was at peace. It was quite a change from noisy, rapidly growing Miami.

The Everglades, seen from Tamiami Trail, April, 1950

Marjory's responsibilities at the paper kept getting larger. There were constant deadlines. After a time, the pressure of the job became too much for her. It was no longer fun. She was tired and became ill. In 1924, at the age of 34, her doctor ordered her to leave the paper and rest for a while.

Naturally, Frank and Lilla worried about her. Frank was also disappointed since he had hoped Marjory would become the newspaper's editor when he retired. Lilla, as always, was helpful and understanding. Marjory rested quietly in their home and tried to get well.

As soon as she felt a little better, she began writing again. This time she sent stories about Florida to some of the many new magazines which were started after the end of World War I. Editors were interested in her articles and stories since so many people were moving to sunny, warm Florida. She knew a lot about the southern part of the state and quickly found buyers for her writing. She sold some stories to the *Saturday Evening Post*, one of the most popular magazines of the day. Marjory was happy when she realized that she could support herself from her writing.

Knowing she could earn a living, Marjory thought about a home of her own. She imagined how she would want it to look.

Marjory joined some friends in buying a small piece of land in Coconut Grove, a community southwest of Miami. Many artists and writers had settled there. Marjory dreamed about building a little "workshop" for herself on her property. She wanted her home to have one large room where she could live and write. Of course, bookcases would have to line its walls. She also wanted a small spare room and a bathroom. Since Marjory seldom cooked, the kitchen could be tiny. Since she had never learned to drive, there was no need for a garage. She also decided she didn't want air–conditioning. She had learned when she first came to Florida that in the south:

You didn't live in the house,
you lived on the porch,
you lived in the outdoors
with the lovely air
blowing in all the windows.

After much thought, her plans for her very own little cottage were perfect. She would soon be sitting on the steps outside her home with a cat nearby.

Marjory on her Doorstep
Coconut Grove

Marjory at Home
Coconut Grove

Marjory would live in her home
with her cats for over 70 years.
It was in this wonderful workshop
that she entertained her friends
and wrote and dreamed
of ways to make south Florida
a better place. It was here that
she thought about the Florida Everglades
and ways to protect them
through her writing and speeches.

Chapter 8.

New Challenges

When Marjory was better, the building of her home began. Her small house was finished in 1926, when Marjory was 36 years old. Shortly before moving in, Marjory made a trip to Taunton to see her mother's relatives. On her return to Florida, she packed up her clothing and books. Since she had almost no furniture, friends gave or lent her some. At last, the move was over. She was home. Looking around her living room, lined with bookshelves and books, she commented later:

> I've always had more books than I knew what to do with.

Marjory soon became an active member of the Coconut Grove community. She worked with the Coconut Grove Slum Clearance Committee, which was trying to improve living conditions for the poor. Among other things, laws were soon passed that required all houses to have indoor plumbing. The committee started a loan fund of several thousand dollars so needy people could improve their own homes and slowly pay back the money they had borrowed to make improvements. The group continued its work for many years under the name "Coconut Grove Cares," always working for better schools and homes, and fighting against the use of drugs. People knew that Marjory was always ready to work for a cause that would help make south Florida a better place to live.

Dr. David Fairchild was known to many people in Miami and around the world. He was a 'plant explorer.' Working for the plant and seed department of the United States Department of Agriculture, David and his wife, Marian, traveled throughout the world. David was also concerned about the Everglades and, as early as 1930, he became the president of what was then known as the Tropical Everglades Park Association. David would soon offer Marjory a writing opportunity that would change her life.

About this time another Miami resident, Colonel Robert Montgomery, decided to create a tropical botanical garden in Miami. He asked David, one of the world's most important plant explorers, to become involved in the garden's development. They felt it should become a place where people could visit to enjoy a world class collection of rare and unusual trees and plants. As the beautiful garden was being planned, David realized there should be a way to tell the public about it. He asked Marjory to write a short pamphlet explaining why the garden was important, why it was being developed, and what visitors would find there.

The research on this pamphlet and another that she would write later on the *Joys of Bird Watching in Florida* gave her wonderful information and contacts. Through her writing, she also developed a better understanding of the natural world. It was knowledge she would use for years to come in her writing and her speeches.

When Marjory finished the 23–page pamphlet, everyone was pleased. It contained a great deal of interesting information. It also had a long name: *An Argument for a Tropical Botanical Garden in South Florida.* The garden would formally be named the Fairchild Tropical Garden. The pamphlet Marjory wrote was read by many people in the state and far beyond. It, and the many speeches she gave, helped gain support for the garden.

The Fairchild Tropical Garden was the only garden of its kind in North America. There was much excitement when it opened. Because she had written the pamphlet, Marjory was asked to speak about it, often at garden clubs. She made many speeches about the garden before and after its opening. At first she was nervous speaking in front of large groups of people. But that soon passed. She may have remembered her days at Wellesley when she was told to holler to the back of the auditorium. Marjory found that she enjoyed speaking as much as she enjoyed writing.

Life was almost perfect. Marjory had many friends in south Florida. She enjoyed her home in Coconut Grove, and she supported herself with her writing. In addition to magazine articles, she also wrote short stories and plays. One of her plays, *The Gallows Gate*, won prizes in state and national competitions. Marjory began to think about writing a novel, a longer story, about Miami and its growth.

In 1938, Marjory's Aunt Fanny, one of her last relatives on her mother's side, died in Taunton. Marjory traveled north to empty the family home and put it up for sale. It was a sad time filled with many memories. The money left to her by her aunt was enough to pay off the mortgage on her little Coconut Grove home.

In 1941, Marjory's father, Frank Bryant Stoneman, died when he was 84. Frank also left his daughter a little money. Although it wasn't much, Marjory was determined to do something special with it—something important as a way to remember her father who had made such a difference to her and to the people of Miami.

She thought and thought about how she could honor her father. Now 51, she finally decided it was time to write her novel. She would use the money her father left her to support herself while she wrote the novel, her story of Miami's growth.

Chapter 8.

Everglades: River Or Swamp?

Marjory had been working on her novel for only a short time when a friend and fellow author came to visit. Hervey Allen was editor of a series of books about America's rivers. He asked if Marjory would like to write about the Miami River.

Marjory talked with Hervey about the idea. She told Hervey that the Miami River was short and she thought its water came from the Everglades. She asked if it would be possible to write about the Everglades instead. Hervey and his publisher agreed.

Because of the Everglades project, Marjory put aside her work on the Miami novel. She began to research the Everglades. Although she didn't know it then, the Everglades would be an important part of the rest of her life. Marjory studied everything she could find about the Everglades. She wanted her book to help people understand the importance of the unusual Everglades.

Marjory had been in the Everglades before. She enjoyed the wildlife and the wildness of the area. She knew the area was wet and watery, but what was the Everglades? Was it a river? Was it swampland? With most rivers, people can jump in and swim. The Everglades was so shallow that, in a lot of places, if you jumped in you would sink knee–deep into the mud. She knew that water in other rivers moved quickly, but the water in the Everglades flowed very, very slowly. The water looked like it was not flowing at all.

Marjory had many questions. She needed answers before she could begin to write. Her first stop was a visit with John D. Pennekamp. He was a friend who had taken her father's place at the *Herald*. John knew so much about nature. He shared his thoughts about the importance of the Everglades. Years later, he was honored when the only underwater park in the United States was named

for him. The John Pennekamp Coral Reef State Park is located near Key Largo, Florida. It extends seven miles into the Atlantic Ocean and protects over 650 species of fish.

John suggested that Marjory see Florida's expert on water, Gerry Parker. Marjory asked *John D. Pennekamp, 1967*

Gerry the same question. Exactly what were the Everglades? River? Swamp? Or something else?

Gerry said the water, although it was flowing ever so slowly, was moving. Therefore, by definition, the Everglades was a river. In order to help Marjory learn more about the area, Gerry gave her a detailed map.

Marjory pinned that map up on her door. She studied it carefully. She began to understand that the Everglades was a sheet of running water that flows from Lake Okeechobee toward the Ten Thousand Islands in south Florida. She saw that ridges on either side hold the water in the central part of the state. After looking at the map for a long time, she understood why the Everglades was a river.

Marjory was still puzzled. The Everglades was a river that didn't look like a river. She needed, in just a few words, to explain that curious fact in the title of her book. She remembered the Indians had called the area *pa–hay–okee*, or grassy waters. She asked Gerry:

> *Do you think I could get away with calling it the river of grass?*

Gerry agreed that "river of grass" would be a good way to describe the Everglades. Later, experts said that by those three words, "river of grass," Marjory began to educate people.

During the almost five years she spent researching and writing her book, Marjory often worked with Gerry Parker. She also asked seemingly endless questions at the United States Soil Conservation Service and at the Florida Everglades Experiment Station. She always took careful notes.

Another person she went to see was Ernest F. Coe, a landscape architect from the north who was particularly interested in the Everglades. He believed they were a national treasure and should become a national park. Ernest devoted his life to trying to protect the Everglades. He was a key

person responsible for lobbying for what we now know as Everglades National Park. Marjory was also a member of the first committee to work toward that becoming a reality. Ernest took Marjory on many trips into the Everglades and taught her about the water, the grasses,

Ernest Coe, April, 1929

and the wildlife. She sometimes went out on the grassy river in a canoe or a motorboat.

Marjory questioned everything. No matter how many answers she found, those answers always seemed to lead to more and more questions. After three years of studying the Everglades and asking every question she could think of, Marjory was finally ready to begin to write her book. By this time, she understood the Everglades better than most other people in the world.

When she started putting her notes together, she realized the first sentence of her book would be very important. Again, she wanted to convince people that the Everglades were unique, very different from other rivers of the world. She chose these words:

There are no other Everglades in the world. They are, they have always been, one of the unique regions of the earth, remote, never wholly known. Nothing anywhere else is like them . . .

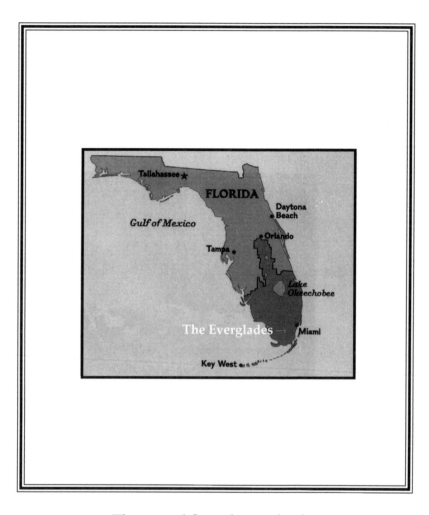

The natural flow of water for the
Greater Everglades Ecosystem
began south of Orlando in the Kissimmee River Valley
and flowed slowly into Lake Okeechobee.
The shallow sheet of water known as
the Everglades traveled from Lake Okeechobee
south to the Gulf of Mexico and Florida Bay.

Chapter 9.

The Everglades: River Of Grass

As Marjory wrote, she told the history of the fascinating wetlands in south Florida. She talked about the Spanish mapmakers, long ago, who named the area *El Laguno del Espiritu Santo*, which means *The Lagoon of the Blessed Spirit*. On their early 1700s maps, English mapmakers called it *River Glades*. To those mapmakers, the word glade meant "shining" or "bright" or "a clear place in the sky." Still later, soon after the United States acquired Florida from Spain, the Turner map of 1823 first used the term *Everglades* to describe the area.

In her book, Marjory explained the Everglades in clear and easy to understand words. She wrote that before man tried to change the flow in the 1800s, the water for the Everglades came from rains. Those rains fell not only in the Everglades, but also in central and south Florida, starting around the Disney World area near Kissimmee. The Kissimmee River slowly took the flow of water to large, flat, saucer–shaped Lake Okeechobee, farther south. The water coming in would make the lake fill or even overflow. The natural overflow would head south as a gently moving, wide, shallow sheet of water, called the Everglades. The sheet of water in places was 50, 60, or even 70 miles wide.

It flowed south from Lake Okeechobee for about 100 miles to empty, ever so slowly, into Florida Bay and the Gulf of Mexico.

Marjory wrote about people who had lived in the Everglades. Long ago, the Calusa Indians made their homes in the western area. The Jeaga and the Tequesta Indians lived along the east coast of Florida. The Mayaimi Indians were closer to Lake Okeechobee. Then the name of the lake was "Mayaimi, " which meant *wide*, but the name was later changed to Okeechobee which means *big water*. All of these Indian tribes—the Calusa, the Jeaga, the Tequesta, and the Mayaimi—depended on the Everglades for food, clothing, and tools.

By the 1800s, Seminole Indians, and what are now called Miccosukee Indians, came to live in the Everglades to escape from United States Army troops. As a result of the Seminole Indian Wars, the troops tried to move the Seminoles west in the 1830s and 1840s. The Indians quickly moved from one place to another in dugout canoes they made from trees that grew in the Everglades. They were often able to outsmart the troops by hiding in the Everglades' water, thick trees, and grasses.

The first white settlers found mosquitoes, snakes, and alligators. Then, as now, there were just two seasons in the Everglades—wet or dry. The land was covered with water or was dried up like caked, parched mud. It was hard for the settlers to clear land to grow crops. Saw grass was everywhere. Time and again they cut themselves and their clothing on the sharp–edged grass. Some hoped to drain water off the land so they could plant in the rich, black earth underneath. *Grasses*

Marjory learned and wrote about everything she saw or heard about the Everglades. For example, she found that saw grass was not really a

grass. It was one of the world's oldest growing plants. The more she discovered, the more fascinated she was by the mysterious Everglades. *Everglades, 1954*

She explored the Big Cypress area to see the magnificent cypress trees. In some watery areas, small tree–islands, known as bay–heads or hammocks, rise up from the watery muck. Marjory saw mangroves and learned about their unusual ability to make new islands or expand old ones with their spreading root systems.

Corkscrew Cypress Swamp, 1958

Marjory learned how many kinds of animals, birds, and fish had adapted to living in the slow–moving water. From panthers to the red–shouldered hawk and the brown deer, all depended on the proper, natural flow of water for survival.

Unfortunately, beginning in the 1800s, many people wanted to change what was natural about the Everglades. In the last few chapters of her book, Marjory told about the efforts that had been made to change the flow of the water. Marjory decided that her last chapter would have to be called the "Eleventh Hour."

The chapter was a warning for readers. She wrote that "the Everglades were dying." Building programs had changed the natural flow of water. Cities and farms were booming, but nobody thought much about what "progress" was doing to the Everglades. A levee and canals were built at the edge of Lake Okeechobee which stopped the natural movement of the water from the lake into the Everglades. Dikes and pumps changed the course of water away from the many new farms in the area. Everything was worked out scientifically. Crops grew quickly. People made money. But what about the egret and the white ibis and the alligator? What about the saw grass that was burned? What about the Indians living in the Everglades?

There was some hope. In 1928, Ernest F. Coe had the idea to make the Everglades into a national park. In 1946, Florida's Governor Millard Caldwell set up an Everglades National Park Commission to secure land for such a park. Finally in 1947, Everglades National Park became a reality.

President Harry S Truman dedicates Everglades National Park for the "Enrichment of the Human Spirit," December 6, 1947

Her book was complete. Marjory and others attended the ceremony and knew the first step toward preserving at least part of the Everglades had been accomplished.

After almost five years of research and writing, it would be fair to say that Marjory understood the Everglades. She warned people, just as her father had done years before, that changing the natural flow of water in the Everglades could endanger the wildlife and plants, as well as the people living in south Florida.

Although many people had helped her to learn about the Everglades, Marjory chose to dedicate her book:

To the memory of my father, who gave me Florida.

The Everglades: River of Grass, was published in November, 1947, just a month before Everglades National Park opened. Her publisher printed 7,500 copies of Marjory's book and they all sold within one month. More copies were printed as quickly as possible. The book is so full of information that it is still in print today, over 50 years later.

Marjory had no idea at that time what changes the Everglades and her book would make in her life. When she put away the research materials after her Everglades book was published, Marjory probably thought she would move on to other things. There was no way she could know then that she would spend years fighting to protect the Everglades.

Marjory Autographs
First Edition Copies of
The Everglades: River of Grass
at Burdine's Department Store
Miami, Florida, November, 1947

< Marjory loved books from the time she was a child. Picture shows her holding a book at a Miami Library Bookmobile that carried books to readers, ca. 1940s

Marjory holds a Wake Up and Read Poster promoting National Library Week at the Jacksonville Public Library

Chapter 10.

Her Writing Continues

After so many years of working on her book about the Everglades, Marjory took a short vacation. She was then ready to continue work on her novel about Miami and its fast growth in the 1920s.

Road to the Sun was published in 1951, when Marjory was 61 years old. By that age, some people would have stopped working to sit in the sun and rest, but not Marjory. It was clear that she was eager to continue writing about Florida.

Her next two projects were books for younger readers. *Freedom River* is the story of three boys, one white, one Miccosukee Indian, and one an escaped slave, who lived at the time that Florida became a state in 1845. *Alligator Crossing* is an adventure story set in Everglades National Park. Both were written as part of two series of books for teenagers.

Over the years, Marjory met many other writers. Some of her favorite writing friends lived in Florida and also wrote about the changes that were happening in the state. One of these people was Marjorie Kinnan Rawlings, who lived at Cross Creek in north central Florida. Both women had come to Florida from the north. While Marjorie

wrote about the Florida Crackers, people who lived in central Florida, Marjory wrote about places in south Florida. They had much in common and enjoyed visiting, writing, and talking with each other.

Marjorie Kinnan Rawlings
< at Cross Creek, ca. 1940

Another "Marjorie" friend was Marjorie Harris Carr, who lived on a farm near Micanopy, Florida, not far from Cross Creek. In 1962, she heard that a Cross Florida Barge Canal was planned. In 1969, Marjorie and a group of her friends founded Florida Defenders of the Environment. Instead of a barge canal, the area became the Cross Florida Greenway and, in 1998, it was named in honor of Marjorie Harris Carr. Here was another good person working to save the Florida environment in another part of the state.

Marjorie Harris Carr at the
Ocklawaha River, 1966 >

52

Marjory kept writing. In 1958, when she was 68, *Hurricane* was published. The research for that book took her all over Florida and into several other states and their islands along the East Coast.

Lilla had a rich knowledge of Florida's history. She helped with the research for *Florida: The Long Frontier*. It was published in 1967, when Marjory was 77 years old. Marjory called it a "pop, non–textbook history." The book, in a readable way, told the fascinating story of Florida from its very beginnings.

Even when researching and writing, Marjory was active in her community. If she learned of

something that needed to be done, she stepped forward and spoke out for what she believed was right. For example, she helped the Seminole and Miccosukee Indians settle a claim for land from the United States Government. Marjory traveled to Washington, D.C. and was ready to speak in front of the Indian Claims Commission.

Marjory with a Miccosukee Indian in the Everglades, 1965

Although the case was decided in favor of the Indians before it was her turn to speak, people knew they could depend on Marjory to speak up for what she felt was right.

But life for Marjory was not all research, writing, and speaking out. It was not all work, by any means. She had many friends and danced and swam until she was in her late 70s. Even when her eyesight was dimmed and she could no longer read, she continued her lifelong interest in books and the written word. It was impossible to keep Marjory from her beloved books. She often borrowed audio book cassette tapes from the Library of Congress in Washington, D.C. and became one of their best customers. Marjory loved to discuss books she "heard" with friends who came to visit.

With all her accomplishments, Marjory could have relaxed when she approached the age of 80. But there were *still* things for her to do. Little did Marjory know that one of the most important chapters in her life was about to begin. Something dreadful was about to happen to the Everglades.

Quickly and unexpectedly, she heard the news. Plans had been made to build a giant jetport in the Everglades. Could it be that the 'Eleventh Hour' Marjory had written about in *The Everglades: River of Grass* was about to begin?

Chapter 11.

Friends of the Everglades

*F*or many years, Marjory was aware of just about everything that was happening in the Everglades. She knew that people had learned from her father's writings. She believed they had learned from Ernest Coe's efforts to create the Everglades National Park. She was often told that her book helped emphasize the importance of the Everglades. But she would soon realize that none of this had been enough. The idea of creating new canals, new developments, new towns, and new roads in the Everglades had stayed in the minds of developers.

Marjory and many other south Florida residents were stunned and upset when the giant jetport building project was suddenly announced. There had been almost no talk of the project. The public was not closely involved in any of the planning process. People simply woke up one morning to hear that the largest jetport in the world was going to be built in "their" Everglades.

Planes were expected to take off or land every 30 seconds. In addition, people were told that a new highway would be built to connect the jetport with nearby cities. And, because of the good roads and air transportation that would be created, thinking was already underway for a new city in the Everglades.

The building project would have blocked the flow of water into Everglades National Park. It would have destroyed forever the wetlands in the center of south Florida. It seemed that no one had thought about the animals, or the plants, or the importance of the Everglades in providing the water supply for south Florida.

People were concerned. Some became furious when they learned that the building plans had been quickly and quietly approved by the area's officials. It had happened so quickly that the citizens hardly knew what to do. To make matters worse, as soon as the plans were approved, bulldozers appeared and started to knock down palm trees. The wet lands were going to be paved over. The developers were on the move.

Something had to be done–and fast. Who would lead the fight against this mass destruction? Who would speak out for the endangered birds and animals? Who would speak for the river of grass? Groups of people started doing what they could, but their efforts were not enough.

Where was Marjory? These were her Everglades, too.

One day, very soon after the plans were announced, she was in a grocery store. While there, Marjory met a woman who was working to defeat the jetport. Marjory congratulated her on the work being done. The younger woman looked straight at Marjory and asked how Marjory, now almost 80, was helping. Marjory reminded the woman that she had written a book about the Everglades. "That's not enough," she was told. More workers of all ages were needed if they hoped to stop the jetport.

Marjory knew the words were true. She had to do something, but how could she, at her age, *again* help to save the Everglades? Joe Browder, then the head of the Audubon Society in Miami, suggested that Marjory start a group that could work to save the Everglades. Marjory sat at home, surrounded by her books. She considered what she could do. Marjory may have thought about her father and all her relatives who had accomplished worthwhile things. She may have thought about all the other people she had known throughout her long lifetime who had spoken up for what they believed was right. She knew that when people got together they could accomplish mighty things. After puzzling for some time, Marjory had an idea. She thought it was a good idea. But, would it work?

She decided to test the idea. At a party, called a Ramble, at Fairchild Tropical Garden, she told

Michael Chenoweth about her plan to start a group called the Friends of the Everglades. She thought it should be an organization that would be open to all people and that anyone could join. Michael listened carefully as she described the idea for the Friends of the Everglades and reached into his wallet. He thought the cost of membership should be very little—perhaps just $1. "I think it's a great idea," he said. Marjory was handed $1. The Friends of the Everglades had its first member. The year was 1969 and Michael has been an active member ever since.

Soon there were more than 3,000 Friends of the Everglades in over 35 states and today there are over 6,000 members around the world. Marjory told many groups, large and small, about what they could do to help. It was true that she couldn't see well, but she could hear and she could certainly speak about the Everglades and their importance. Joe Podgor, Marjory's good friend, emphasized:

> The Everglades is a test—if we pass it, we get to keep the planet.

The Everglades was now more than an interest to Marjory. At over 80 years of age, saving the Everglades became a passion. Perhaps everything that had gone before in her lifetime had just been leading up to her final "holler to the back of the auditorium." Marjory spoke plainly and clearly about preserving the Everglades. Not all audiences wanted to hear what Marjory had to say. She was not always welcome. Marjory commented that:

No matter how poor my eyes are, I can still talk. I'll talk about the Everglades at the drop of a hat. Whoever wants me to talk, I'll come over and tell them about the necessity of preserving the Everglades. Sometimes I tell them more than they wanted to know.

Soon, other members of the Friends of the Everglades began to make speeches, too. In fact, the group became so strong and important that the Friends of the Everglades was sometimes called "Marjory's Army." They, along with many others, were able to block construction of the jetport. It was an important day for the people of south Florida when that project was defeated.

Although there would be no jetport, the Friends of the Everglades knew they had to be on guard. Many people worked together to share

knowledge and support. Art Marshall, who had learned much about the water in south Florida, helped the Friends and others scientifically understand the need for protecting the Everglades.

Marjory Speaks for the Friends of the Everglades, with Florida ecologist, Arthur Marshall, 1972–73

Much has been accomplished to try to restore the Everglades, but much still needs to be done. Everglades National Park is now recognized by the world as a critically important area to the life of our planet. It has been designated an International Biosphere Reserve, a World Heritage Site, and a Ramsar Convention Wetland of International Importance. However, Everglades National Park only includes part of the original Everglades. Florida is now in the process of restudying how to restore and reclaim even more of the Everglades.

The restoration will take a lot of work. The panther, which was elected by schoolchildren to be the state animal of Florida, lives in the Everglades and is endangered. The natural flow of water is so controlled by canals and dams and other man–

made water control devices, that even the pro-tected Everglades National Park is in danger.

So many of the birds that lived in the natural Everglades already are gone or are endangered because changes in water levels affect their nesting habits. The natural flow of the water is also critical for the amount of clean drinking water in south Florida.

Great Egret in the Everglades

Even at over 100 years of age, Marjory continued to speak out for the protection of the Everglades. Now, the Friends of the Everglades and its children's arm, Young Friends of the Everglades—called *"Majory's Echo,"* continue her work.

Marjory Stoneman Douglas celebrated her 108th birthday on April 7, 1998, and died a little more than a month later, on May 14th. Friends gathered to remember her at Everglades National Park. At the time of her death, Marjory, at 108, had been the oldest living member of the original committee to create Everglades National Park. Although her work was over, her words will not be forgotten. One of the statements that Marjory often made was that:

Our biggest problem now is that there are so many people coming to Florida who don't understand the fragile nature of the land. People need to be educated about the environment in order to understand and appreciate it.

To "live in harmony with nature" is sometimes hard to do. It is tempting to try to change what nature has created. Those words that she learned so long ago in her geography class at Wellesley College are still important to remember. Marjory Stoneman Douglas certainly helped us all, through her words and writing, to learn the necessity of living in harmony with nature.

Marjory didn't start out to save anything. She simply spoke out for what she believed to be right. A newspaper article in the Tampa *Tribune* at the time of her death said it so well:

She may have lost her sight, but she refused to surrender her vision.

Marjory Stoneman Douglas who often reminded us, "Let's Get On With It!"

Afterword

$\mathcal{F}$or her writing about the Everglades and her active willingness to speak out, Marjory Stoneman Douglas was named Conservationist of the Year by the Florida Audubon Society in 1975. In 1976, the Florida Wildlife Federation honored her with their Conservationist of the Year Award.

When Marjory was 90, Dade County (now Miami–Dade County), the Florida county where Miami and part of the Everglades are located, created Marjory Stoneman Douglas Day. It is celebrated each year on her birthday, April 7th.

When she was 93, she was named to the Florida Women's Hall of Fame. In Key Biscayne, Florida, it will soon be possible to visit the Marjory Stoneman Douglas Biscayne Nature Center

In 1985, when Marjory was 95 years old, she was awarded the National Parks and Conservation Association's first Citizen Conservation Award— which is also named for her.

Also in 1985, the State of Florida formally recognized her. A state office building in Tallahassee was named the Marjory Stoneman Douglas Building. The building houses the Florida Department of Natural Resources, that part of state gov-

ernment most responsible for protecting the environment. In 1987, at age 97, Marjory was named a "Great Floridian" for her work to protect the important Florida Everglades and for being the Founder of the Friends of the Everglades.

In 1993, the President of the United States awarded the Presidential Medal of Freedom to Marjory. It is America's highest civilian award. During the presentation, President William Clinton called her "the Grandmother of the Everglades" and said that she was:

Legendary . . . an inspiration to generations of conservationists.

In 1997, when Marjory was 107 years old, federal funding was proposed that would help preserve the Everglades. A 1.3 million acre wilderness in the Everglades National Park has been named the "Marjory Stoneman Douglas Wilderness."

When the area was dedicated, Joette Lorion, President of the Friends of the Everglades said:

There would be no more fitting recognition than to name these still wild areas of the priceless Everglades National Park after Marjory Stoneman Douglas. Henry David Thoreau reminded us that "in wildness is the preservation of the world." It is equally true that in wildness is the preservation of the Everglades. We believe that Marjory Stoneman Douglas's name on this beautiful wilderness area will help preserve her beloved "River of Grass" for generations to come.

Friends remember Marjory at the door of her Coconut Grove cottage, greeting them, ready to share her ideas about the Everglades. Plans are now underway to protect the cottage, which was her home for 72 years.

Marjory at Home, Coconut Grove

Chronology

This chronology describes some of the important events in the life of Marjory Stoneman Douglas and her age when they occurred.

In the year	Marjory was	And this happened
1890		Marjory is born in Minneapolis, Minnesota
1895	5	Marjory and her mother move to Taunton, Massachusetts to live with her grandparents.
1912	22	Marjory graduates from Wellesley College. Later that year, her mother dies.
1914	24	Marjory marries Kenneth Douglas, but the marriage does not last.
1915	25	Marjory moves to Miami, Florida to be near her father and his second wife. Her writing career begins at the Miami *Herald*.
1916-20	26-30	Marjory serves in the war effort, first with the Naval Reserves and then with the American Red Cross in France and other parts of Europe.
1920	30	Marjory returns to Miami and the *Herald*.
1926	36	Marjory moves into her Coconut Grove home. There she writes stories, articles, books, and speeches. She will live in the small cottage with her cats for the rest of her life.
1947	57	Everglades National Park is dedicated and *The Everglades: River of Grass* is published.
1969	79	*Friends of the Everglades* is created to fight against a jetport which was proposed to be built in the Everglades.
1984	94	The State of Florida's Department of Natural Resources Building was named for her.
1993	103	Marjory is awarded the Medal of Freedom by the President of the United States who calls her the "Grandmother of the Everglades."
1997	107	Over a million acres of the Everglades are formally named the Marjory Stoneman Douglas Wilderness Area.
1998	108	Marjory Stoneman Douglas dies.

Glossary

ANCESTORS — The people from whom one is descended, such as parents, grandparents, great-grandparents, etc.

DEADLINE — A date by which something must be done.

EDITOR — The person who prepares work for publication, such as in a newspaper, magazine, book, etc.

ENVIRONMENT — All the combined factors (such as soil, climate, and living things), that must be present in order for a plant or animal to survive.

EVERGLADES — A low lying area of swampy or marshy land: a river of grass.

FRONTIER — An area that forms the border between a settled area and the wilderness.

JETPORT — An airport for jet airplanes.

MANGROVES — Tropical trees that live in or near the water and send out many roots which form dense, bushy thickets.

MUCK — Dark, rich soil.

UNIQUE — Very unusual, the only one of its kind.

WETLANDS — Areas, such as swamps, which contain a great deal of moisture.

*Marjory Stoneman Douglas,
ca. 1940s*

Index

—A—

Allen, Hervey, 37
Alligator Crossing, 51
Alligators, 29, 47
American Red Cross, 25-26
An Argument for a Tropical Botanical Garden in South Florida, 35
Atlantic Ocean, 38

—B—

Browder, Joe, 57
Burdine's Department Store, 49

—C—

Caldwell, Millard, 47
Calusa Indians, 44
Carr, Marjorie Harris, 52
— Cross Florida Greenway, 52
Chenoweth, Michael, 58
China, 12
Civil War, 10
Clinton, William, 64
Coe, Ernest F., 40, 47, 55
Coffin
— Kate, 10
— Levi, 10
Corkscrew Cypress Swamp, 46
Cross Florida Barge Canal, 52
Cuba, Havana, 11

—D—

Dartt, Miss, Marjory's teacher, 14
Deer, Brown, 46
Disney World, 43
Douglas

— Kenneth, 17-18
— Marjory Stoneman, 3-4, 8, 17, 19-20, 22-41, 43-46, 48-65
— Biscayne Nature Center, 63
— Building, 63
— Day, 63
— Wilderness, 64

—E—

East Coast, 53
Egret, 47, 61
Eleventh Hour, 46, 54
Eppes, Francis, 20
Europe, 12
Everglades: River of Grass, The, 3-4, 48-49

—F—

Fairchild
— David, 27, 34
— Marian, 27, 34
— Tropical Garden, 35, 57
Flagler, Henry, 20-21, 24
Florida, 11, 21, 23-24, 28, 30, 33, 43, 51, 53, 60, 62-63
— Audubon Society, 57, 63
— Conservationist of the Year, 63
— Bay, 42, 44
— Big Cypress, 46
— Central, 43, 52
— Coconut Grove, 3, 31-33, 35-36, 65
— Cares, 33
— Slum Clearance Committee, 33
— Crackers, 52

Books to Read to Learn More

Marjory Stoneman Douglas: Voice of the River, with John Rothchild

The Everglades, River of Grass, by Marjory Stoneman Douglas

Freedom River, by Marjory Stoneman Douglas

Photographic Credits

Florida Photographic Collection, Florida State Archives for all images except the following:

David Carr for the image of Marjorie Harris Carr

Claudine Laabs for the cover images of Marjory Stoneman Douglas and Great Egrets

What You Can See and Do Today

Become a member of the *Friends of the Everglades*. You, too, can join over 6,000 volunteers. If you are an adult, the minimum fee is $10. If you are a youngster, join *Marjory's Echo,* the Young Friends of the Everglades section of the organization for $1. Contact the *Friends of the Everglades* at 7800 Red Road, Suite 215K, Miami, Florida. Phone: (305) 669-0858.

Everglades National Park. The main park entrance is about 10 miles southwest of Homestead-Florida City on Route 9336. The Marjory Stoneman Douglas Wilderness of 1.3 million acres is part of the Park. For details, hours, and fees, please phone: 305-242-7700.

The *University of Miami's Richter Library* in Coral Gables, Florida contains many of Marjory Stoneman Douglas' personal papers.

The Marjory Stoneman Douglas Home at 3744 Stewart Avenue, Coconut Grove will become a state historic home.

The Fairchild Tropical Garden, 10901 Old Cutler Road, Miami, Florida 33156, (305) 667-1651, is open daily from 9:30-4:30. Before the garden opened, Marjory wrote about it. Before and after it opened, she spoke to many groups to develop interest in the Fairchild Tropical Garden.

Other Books in the Southern Pioneer Series

The Southern Pioneer Series has been developed to provide easy to read books about remarkable people and places that have shaped Florida's history. Titles include:

Jacqueline Cochran, America's Fearless Aviator. The story of a poor child of the Florida Panhandle who, through determination and skill, became one of the most important aviators in American history. ISBN 0-9631241-6-1, paperback, $14.95.

Henry Flagler, Builder of Florida. The beautifully told story of a boy who left home at the age of 14 to make a fortune—and made two. First a partner in Standard Oil, he then brought tourism to Florida's east coast through railroads, hotels, and more. ISBN 0-9631241-3-7, paperback, $9.95.

Henry Perrine, Plant Pioneer of the Florida Frontier. As a young man, he decided to have a life of adventure and moved to the Illinois Frontier, Mexico, and Indian Key, Florida during the Seminole Wars. Learn about the exciting life, times, and contributions of the almost forgotten Florida plant pioneer. ISBN 0-9631241-7-X, paperback, $14.95.

Marjorie Kinnan Rawlings and the Florida Crackers. Pulitzer Prize winning American author of *The Yearling,* she wrote about Florida's north central backwoods, the Big Scrub country. ISBN 0-9631241-5-3, paperback, $14.95.

Please contact the Southern Pioneer Series at Tailored Tours Publications, Inc., 800-354-5246, to request a copy of our catalog.